SAVING LESLIE JONES

Saving Leslie Jones

rebirth of spirit in man and horse

TEXT BY DAVE JOSEPH   **PHOTOGRAPHS BY JON KRAL**

FOREWORD BY JANE SMILEY

LONG WIND PUBLISHING

&

First Printing, 2005

Book Design by Jon Ward
Text edited by Beth McLeod and Scott Powers

Saving Leslie Jones; Rebirth of Spirit in Man and Horse
Dave Joseph, 1959- and Jon Kral, 1947-
ISBN 1-892695-16-2
Library of Congress Control Number: 2004095079

Long Wind Publishing, LLC
108 North Depot Drive
Ft. Pierce, FL 34950
www.LongWindPub.com

Printed in Hong Kong

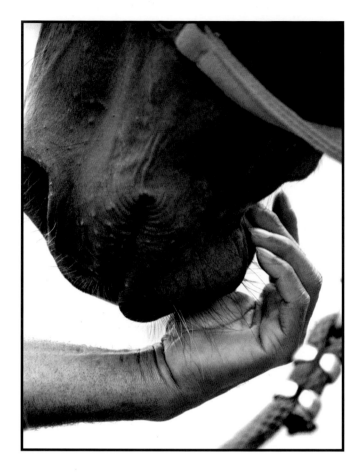

For the women and men I met along the way who inspired me with the passionate ways they act upon their love for these wonderful animals, and for these lucky horses, who-by the way-humbled me as I focused my lens upon them. And to David, without whom I would never have met these people or these horses.

Jon Kral

To the spirit of Theodore C. Joseph and to Hannah Ray . . . the little girl with curly hair.

Dave Joseph

For their invaluable information, inspiration and support, the authors wish to acknowledge the following individuals, with our sincerest apologies for anyone we may have inadvertantly overlooked: Mike Cronin, Diana Pikulski, Melissa Klick, Ellie Jones, Chris Heyde, Shannon Teague, Noreen Carrier (from the film lab), Beth McLeod (for her fine editing), Patti Joseph (for unending support), Scott and Michelle Powers, Jane and Victoria (for the concert), Jim Tremper, J. W. Stephens, Andre Wheeler, Daphne Hewitt and 3 Owls Sheep Dairy, Ed Gray, Bill and Susan Finley, Bittersweet Station, Michele Oren, Kim Wilkins, Fred Turner, Earl Maucker, Kelly and Tracy Young, Betty Jo Bock, Jodi Gray, Linda Miller, Michele Blanco, Chris Lazzarino, Eva Strasser, Christopher Joseph, Pennell Hopkins, George McGrath, Animals' Angels and Lesley Moffat.

CONTENTS

FOREWORD

Thoroughbred horseracing is commonly called an "industry," and is frequently likened to the "entertainment industry." It has a product, racing, and an income stream from betting. Horseracing has stars, whom its special aficionados know and love, such as Bob Baffert and Kelso, and it has its superstars, whom everyone know and love, such as Secretariat, Man O' War and even, for a time, Smarty Jones, who won the Kentucky Derby and the Preakness in 2004. Horseracing and its subsidiary businesses generate a significant chunk of GNP, as horseracing lobbyists never cease telling the legislatures of states where racing is good business: Kentucky, California, New York and Florida. For some fans, horseracing is a passion; for some it is an addiction. Like most industries/passions/addictions, horseracing is fraught with contradictions and is, for that reason, both fascinating and mysterious. Horseracing is a strange and compelling human activity.

But in the kaleidoscope of the human drama of horseracing, the horses themselves have often fallen into oblivion. It takes the thirty-five to forty thousand registered Thoroughbred horses that are born every year to sustain racing in the U. S. (and additional horses, of course, are imported, mostly from Europe and South America). The job of most of these horses, bred though they are to win, is to be also-rans--to fill out racing fields, to give trainers, riders and jockeys something to do, to give bettors an array of choices and to make racing seem populous and exciting. It isn't a bad job, and Thoroughbreds, who are bred to have heart, who are naturally lively and active, for the most part love to do their job. Racetracks all over America are full of not-famous horses who go out every day and try as hard as they can to run as fast as they can for six furlongs or a mile or a mile and a half. Many of them get excellent care and kind handling; others do not. But, if almost all of them were not generous, willing and able, the horseracing "industry" wouldn't be much of an industry at all.

Thoroughbreds race at two, three, four, often five and sometimes six or seven and they usually live into their twenties. Inevitably, they are like high school athletes, who have entire lives to fill after the glory days are over. A few males and rather more females prove themselves on the racetrack and go on to produce the next generation and, in the long term, this system of culling has produced a breed of horses that are generally beautiful and athletic. But many do not prove themselves and it is for those horses that the Thoroughbred Retirement Foundation was formed and now exists. It serves as a conduit for horses out of the racetrack and into new lives. It also serves as a conscience for the industry because we Thoroughbred breeders, owners and trainers must ask ourselves, do we really want those foals we welcomed one fine spring morning, those fillies and colts we watched with such pleasure and hope, to end their lives riding in big double-bottomed cattle trucks to the killers?

A horse is an anamalous animal. It is big and expensive to feed and house, making it a burden in some ways and yet it was domesticated to serve the widest possible variety of human needs and has done so with unique generosity and flexibility. But horses are more than useful--they are friendly and intelligent--their mental capacities, in my view, have hardly been plumbed. Unlike cattle, horses express their individuality every chance they get--in every barn, every herd, every race and every interaction with humans. In today's world, horses have become companion animals, like dogs and cats, and they rise to the occasion with considerable grace, even while they are being produced in an industrial manner, thirty-five thousand per year.

It is to the horse, in all its individual complexity, that the Thoroughbred Retirement Foundation is dedicated. Every horse is named, pondered, made something of. Homes are found. Injuries and illnesses are taken care of. Connections are made that enable each horse to live a useful and valued life. You could even say (as with the title story of Leslie Jones) that therapy is provided. The Foundation has farms in several states and, as of this writing, houses hundreds of horses. It has, in addition, found new homes and new lives for hundreds more over the years. But the benefits conferred on horses are only part of the story. Because of the alliance between the Thoroughbred Retirement Foundation and prisons in a number of states, many people have benefitted too, from being asked to care for and appreciate Thoroughbred horses and finding that their care and appreciation is reciprocated by the animals.

The essays and photographs in this volume show the side of the horse racing industry that is not an industry at all, that is not about winning races and making a profit. As always, with horses, this story is about working hard at tasks that are sometimes uncomfortable and difficult, but it is also about how rewarding that work is when the horses get sleek and happy and the people find their efforts reciprocated a thousandfold by all the many pleasures that horses, especially, in my opinion, Thoroughbred horses, have to give us.

Jane Smiley, author of *Horse Heaven,* et al

PREFACE

The horse: friendship without envy, beauty without vanity, nobility without conceit, a willing partner, yet, no slave." -Anon.

When people learn that I created the Thoroughbred Retirement Foundation over twenty years ago, questions about my background usually come quickly into the discussion. "Was I a horse owner?" "Did I ride?" "Was I a long time horse racing fan?" "Did I grow up around horses or on a farm?" Much to nearly every questioner's surprise, the answer to all of these seemingly logical queries is "No."

How, then, did it all happen? How did a girl from Brooklyn, New York grow to become the founder of the nation's largest and most well-regarded equine rescue organization? And why?

Why, indeed.

The simple answer is, in fact, very simple. Because of my love for horses.

The love of horses is not a birthright. One does not need experience to acquire it. It is not regional or contingent on wins and losses.

It is unconditional and stems from the heart.

This is why that once I learned that the fate of thousands of Thoroughbred horses was at risk each and every year, the decision to act was an easy one.

As expressed in the Koran, *"When God created the horse, He said to the magnificent creature: I have made thee as no other. All treasures of the Earth shall lie between thy eyes. Thou shalt cast thy enemies between thy hooves, but shall carry*

friends upon thy back. Thy saddle shall be the seat of prayers to me. And thy shall fly without any wings, and conquer any sword."

The journey that followed has been well reported and, although the road has sometimes been difficult, we have never faltered.

Today, the Foundation's growth and accomplishments continue at an exhilarating pace. Just as it has been from the very beginning, the fuel behind it all is simply the love of horses.

Perhaps the greatest reward that I have received from my work with the Foundation has been the opportunity to see that love in action. It is on display every day in the work of our many volunteers as they provide care, labor and shelter at our many farms and satellite facilities. We see it from the veterinarians and professionals who donate countless hours to our cause. It is what motivates our farm managers and instructors to choose personal fulfillment over financial reward. It is the supporter who pays from his or her own pocket to save a horse from slaughter by intervening at the auction block. Love is, in fact, the real currency behind every donation we receive, whether large or small.

This sense of love is also found in places one might least expect: at the prisons, detention centers and correctional facilities where Foundation vocational training programs are changing and saving the lives of men and horses alike.

TRF's Maryland farm manager Andre Wheeler shared a touching note from a former juvenile corrections center detainee and vocational training program student, John R., to Wheeler, his mentor at the program:

"Dear Mr. Wheeler,

I just wanted to thank you for letting me work with you. If it is possible, can I get a picture of my horse, Chance? When I get home, I would like to come and see Chance and if it is possible, get a job with you or someone you know. Or maybe, spend my spare time doing some volunteer work for you. I just wanted to thank you for helping me get through my sixty days without getting into trouble. You made me think about all the people in the world that have good hearts. To never think bad about somebody even if they may have done some things wrong in the past, and to always give them a second chance. Thank you!"

Why would anyone be surprised that any man or woman, regardless of background, would want to save a horse? To protect and nurture it? To respect it?

It is not a labor. It is a joy. It is what we must do as concerned, caring and loving human beings.

To all of the thousands who have joined with me in this wonderful calling, you have my deepest heartfelt thanks.

Franz Mairinger said, ". . . the Lord looked down on a Sunday morning and saw that something was missing, something that represented His patience, His understanding, His love, His everything. Indeed, all that was good. And He created the horse."

Monique S. Koehler

"Can you imagine how people who have bred or owned a horse would feel if you took them to (a slaughterhouse) and said, 'Remember that horse who made you $500,000? The one you stood in the grandstand cheering for and spilled a drink on your tie for? The one you led into the Winner's Circle and had your picture taken with? That's him, about to get slammed in the head.'"

Hall of Fame jockey Julie Krone

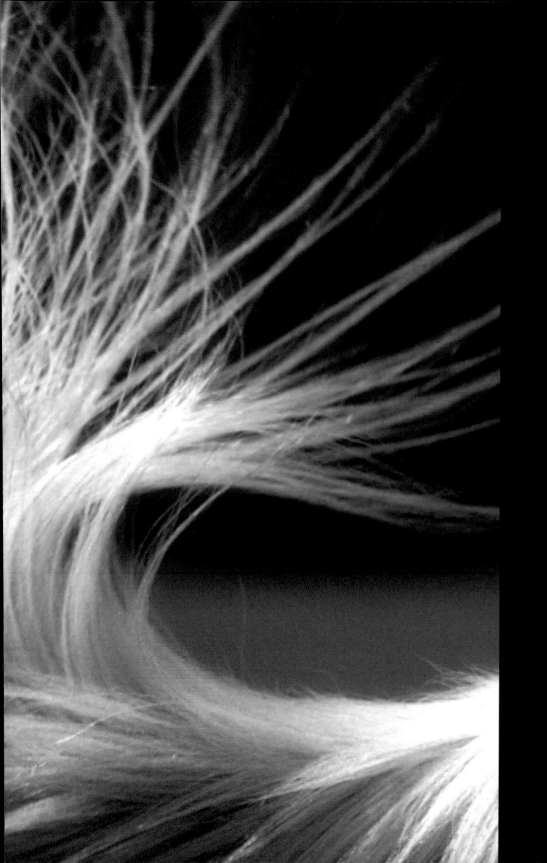

*"Horses will not only give you
teach you how to use them."*

Laura Newberry, President

SAVING LESLIE JONES

She arrived at the Exceller Farm in October when the leaves were turning and there was a hint of winter in Dutchess County. Leslie Jones walked off a van with broken eyes, an indifferent heart and a gray coat covered with painful scabs.

"You could have beaten her with a pole and she probably wouldn't have cared," recalls farm volunteer Melissa Leo. "She had given up." Given up after twenty-three winless races across seven different tracks. A pretty gray filly all beat up and gone to hell. A pretty four-year-old with broken eyes.

"You can tell a lot about a horse from their eyes," said farm manager Michele Oren. She is looking across a field of retired Thoroughbreds at this New York farm. The horses wander along a fence line at their convenience, curious and seeking affection.

"See this one?" Oren asks, holding a young colt. "See how peaceful he is? He is more inquisitive than fearful." She hugs the colt before walking up a dirt path to another field of horses, a field where Leslie Jones stands detached from the others. "But with Leslie . . . there's something that's gone on with her, something that causes her to be on constant alert. I don't know what it is with her eyes. Fear?"

Bred in Canada, Leslie Jones competed for two years. She finished second once; second across a sloppy track in upstate New York. She ended her career having earned $5,137.00. She wasn't a champion and certainly wasn't a horse who could pay her own way or even compete with the lowest class claimers in the country. Maybe she understood that better than anyone because when she arrived at Exceller after being rescued from neglect, Leslie Jones seemed to have lost the will to live.

"She was skin and bones and could barely walk," Leo remembers. "She was in horrible shape. She was sunken in. It was so upsetting and sad."

The filly had abscesses on both front feet and her right knee had an old fracture. Dr. John Jagar, who treated the mare, remembers Leslie Jones suffering from bone damage. And then there was the rain rot, a horrible skin condition that had attached itself to Leslie Jones in the form of disturbing scabs.

"It happens when they're stressed," Jagar explains. "It was very, very painful with her. I recall having to tranquilize her just so she could be bathed."

Leo could see a correlation between Leslie Jones and some of the terminally ill patients she had worked with as a counselor. "There was a hopelessness," she recalls. "In Leslie's eyes you could see she had given up. It's like they turn themselves over to you. They're suffering. They're broken down."

And broken hearted. It took several months to cure the rain rot. And it took a few more before Leslie Jones began to trust the folks at Exceller.

"She's never going to be weight-worthy," Oren says. "She's always going to be a pasture companion, or, as I call it, a pasture ornament. But the way she has slowly turned it around has been very rewarding."

Tentative at first, Leslie Jones walks slowly toward Oren in an open field before dropping her head to graze nearby. Oren looks at the gray mare who still isolates herself from the other horses. "She's had a tough life," she says, reaching over to touch her. "She's come a long way, it's just that . . . I just don't know if those eyes are ever going to change."

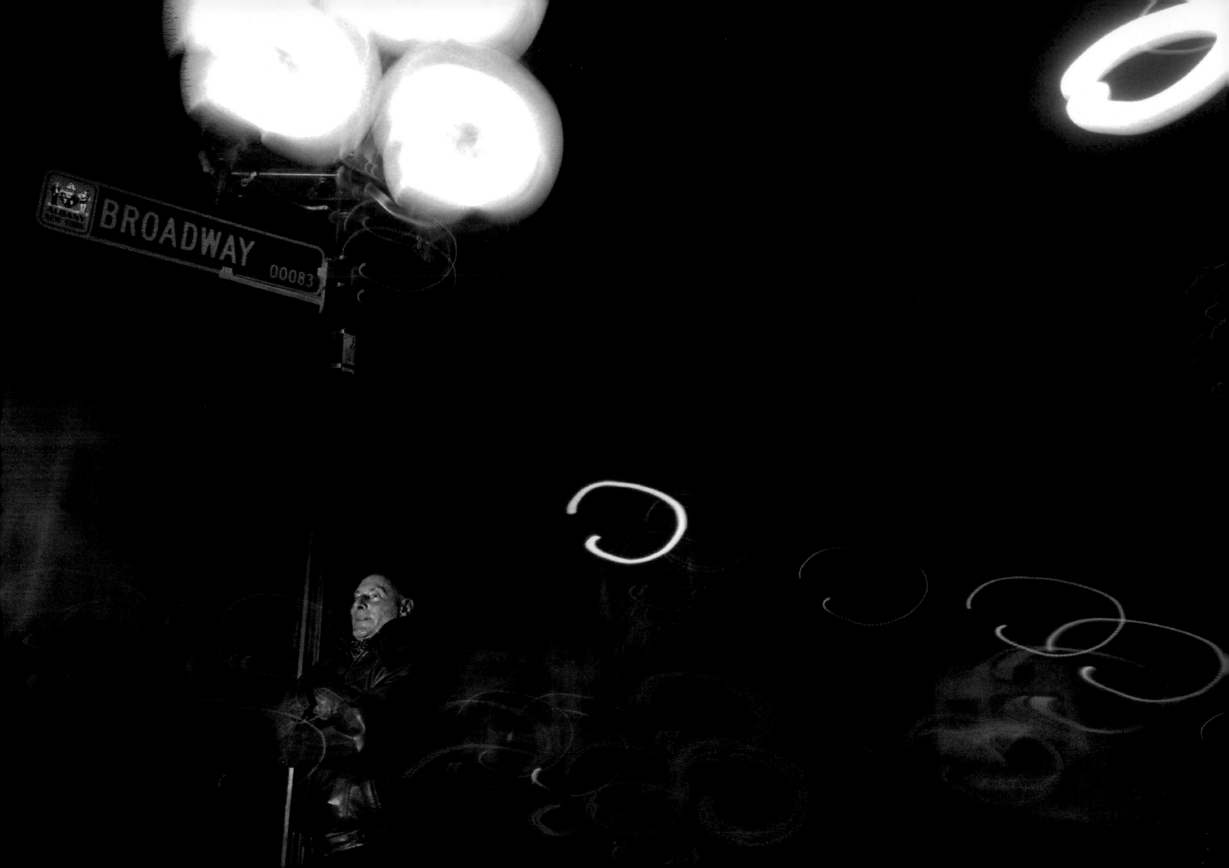

jay

He couldn't process it all those years ago. He admits that now, twenty years removed from living as a homeless junkie on the streets of New York and then as an inmate at Wallkill Correctional Facility. Jay Schleifer couldn't connect the dots. He couldn't drag the line that took him from emotionally crippled to healed.

Heroin doesn't teach virtue and prison doesn't promote freedom. Yet, twenty years later, Schleifer traces his health and rehabilitation to the time he spent on the original crew of inmates who cared for retired Thoroughbreds at Wallkill.

Sipping ginger ale at a corner pub in Albany, N. Y., his face illuminated by a single candle on the small table in front of him, Schleifer says he learned dignity and compassion from the Thoroughbreds at Wallkill. A torn-up junkie learning from beaten-down horses. He smiles at the abstraction.

"It's strange but I look back at the time in my life with great joy and gratitude," he says. "Even though I was in prison I was free."

Schleifer didn't walk into Wallkill with any thoughts of finding solace or rapture. He was a heroin addict; destitute and alone, "living in gutters, literally, and sleeping in abandoned buildings." He ripped off family in Brooklyn. Lied to his friends in the city. "A complete and total junkie," he confesses.

"People ask me what my drug of choice was," Schleifer, 54, adds. "I tell them my drug of choice was anything I could get my hands on. If it works, I'll

take it. But heroin? That was a major addiction."

The addiction made him steal to buy the drugs, and that led to a burglary conviction and three years at Wallkill. For Schleifer, however, his incarceration led him to emotional and physical freedom.

"You have to understand something," he says, fanning the flame while leaning close to the table as if to reveal a secret. "Like me at that time, the horses were alone in the world. Some of the horses were in terrible shape and I was in terrible shape. I related to them. We (inmates) are treated like the outcasts, the misfits of society, and these guys were the misfits of the horse industry. They just didn't fit in anymore. We did it through behavior. It happened to them because they couldn't race anymore. They were neglected through no fault of their own, because they were injured or they couldn't run anymore.

"They didn't fit in and we didn't fit in, so that empathetic bond was there. It was almost automatic. We were both misfits."

Schleifer didn't comprehend the connection at first. "At the time I just thought the horses were cool and they got me out of the penitentiary," he said. "But they were instrumental in my recovery. They gave me a great sense of peace. I didn't feel threatened by them. I felt they loved me and I loved them. It was reciprocal. I could let my guard down with the horses. I didn't have to front like I was a tough guy. The horses were indifferent. They didn't care if you were a tough guy from Brooklyn or someone from the middle of nowhere in cow country. And I felt bad for them, the way some of them were abused. I felt angry, and angry with the people who had done it."

The candle flame dances as another patron enters the bar. After his release from Wallkill, Schleifer took a job working with horses at Belmont Park, then at a riding academy.

"I know Jay had a great experience with the horses," says Father Peter Young, who offered housing and helped rehabilitate Schleifer at his Peter Young Housing, Industries and Treatment program in Albany. "I heard a lot of horse stories over many cups of coffee."

And Schleifer has been telling those stories the past fifteen years of his sobriety.

"Those horses gave me love and tenderness," he adds. "They gave me an opportunity to bond in an emotional way, which is something that my criminal life had completely taken away. Even when I relapsed, I never lost track of the feelings I had for the horses. It was through them I learned to honor the core dignity of a creature, whether it be a four-legged creature or a two-legged creature, because the horses are dignified animals; regal and dignified."

The crowd at the bar is becoming boisterous and night has fallen hard and cold in Albany. Schleifer slips on his leather coat and makes his way to the front door. There's a schedule to keep. He's going to work tomorrow in Johnstown, N.Y.--as an alcohol and substance abuse counselor at the Hale Creek Correctional Facility.

"You got a lot of time to think at night when there's no one to talk to, there's no television and the lights are out. But when you get out with the horses, you don't think about anything but them. You don't think about what happened or why you're here or what went wrong. For a few hours, it's a little getaway."
Inmate Kiayam Ginter with Canadian Connection at Blackburn Correctional Facility, Lexington, KY.

"Even the horses here who haven't won big money still give you one hundred and ten per cent. They give you everything they have. Maybe they didn't have the breeding, maybe they didn't have the heart, but they still gave you everything they had. Now you're just going to throw it aside and start up with another one. And, as soon as he breaks, you're going to do the same thing. To some people they're just freaking money-making machines. Throw it out and get another one. It's like the one I adopted. Who knows what could have happened to her. She could've been steak in Europe."

Wallkill Corrections Officer Greg Petrie, who adopted retired Thoroughbred Foolish Pride.

FROM hELL TO PLEASANT VALLEY

In a village called Pleasant Valley, somewhere off a country road that winds through white, clapboard homes and venerable antique shops, a gelding is galloping along a fence line surrounded by undulating hills and ancient pines.

He is noble and dappled and still fiercely independent at the age of 21. As he breaks into a canter in the shadow of an old red dairy barn, neck bowed and nostrils flaring, Banker's Jet is the perfect ornament to this postcard setting. It is here, on this Connecticut farm owned by Raymond Roy, where you realize every horse should be free to run in the bucolic pastures of Pleasant Valley. Especially one who has been through hell.

"And it was hell," confirms Ron Gibson.

Gibson is seventy now and more than a decade has passed since he first laid eyes on Banker's Jet. But he can't forget his introduction to the gutsy Thoroughbred who earned nearly $700,000 over eight years and competed against the likes of Horse of the Year contender Waquoit.

"You want to know what I remember?" asks Gibson, the former farm manager at Wallkill Correctional Facility, one of several prisons in the country where inmates care for retired Thoroughbreds. "Well, I'll tell you just like it was. It was disgusting. That horse was ready to die. He was skin and bones. He was in a tiny paddock and there was no feed, no water, and the mud in that paddock was so thick and deep it nearly pulled my boots off. Most horses just lay down and die in those conditions. People, too. I guess his guts and courage kept him going."

It was guts and courage that helped carry Banker's Jet through a distinguished racing career. A multiple-stakes winner who competed 106 times across fourteen tracks, Banker's Jet was a model of consistency; winning on dirt and turf, from five furlongs to a 1 3/16th miles. He was Florida's champion sprinter in 1987 and among his victories was the A Phenomenon Handicap at Saratoga.

But the career of Banker's Jet came to an end in September of 1991 when he broke down while finishing third at the Meadowlands. Sore and lame from years at the track---one veterinarian suggested the nine-year-old be put down---Banker's Jet was retired to a farm in upstate New York with the promise that he would be cared for and have a private stall.

But those were hardly the conditions Gibson found when the Thoroughbred Retirement Foundation (TRF) was notified of Banker's Jet's whereabouts and condition. "He was ready to die," Gibson says. "There was no sign of hay, there was no feed tub. I spotted some hay a field away and I gave him most of the whole bale. He looked like he just came out of Auschwitz. He probably weighed around 1,100 pounds when he was racing. He was down to 650-700 pounds when I saw him. I've never seen a horse look much worse who was still alive. I told the folks at the TRF, 'If we don't take him, he'll be dead in two weeks.' "

Shortly after Banker's Jet was rescued, Raymond Roy remembers walking into a drugstore one morning in Pleasant Valley, picking up a newspaper and reading about the gelding's rescue. Roy said the article struck a responsive chord.

"I had visited Jet's sire, Tri Jet, years earlier when we took our children to Disney World and went to Ocala to visit some horse farms," Roy said. "In fact, I still have a picture of me and Tri Jet at Mr. (Fred) Hooper's farm. And as a casual (racing) fan, I'd happened to see Jet race a few times in Boston when we went to the races at Suffolk Downs. So when I read the article about Jet's rescue, it was all a little more pertinent than it might have been otherwise."

Roy adopted Banker's Jet and brought him to Pleasant Valley, along with his pasture companion from Wallkill, Fashion Note. When Fashion Note passed away in 1999 at 34, Roy adopted Angelic Prospect as another companion for Jet.

Roy stands under the eaves of his barn and squints through a steady Sunday morning rain as Banker's Jet calmly grazes in a pasture. Despite leaving the track with fractured splint bones---despite his right ankle being nearly twice the size it should be---Banker's Jet is healthy and safe.

"He's in pretty good condition for his age," Roy said. "He's a high-strung horse, but I've been told by people who were associated with him earlier in his racing career that he was always a hyper horse and relatively difficult to handle. I think that's probably why he got into the trouble he did when they found him. I suspect he wound up on some dude ranch, gave some handler a hard time, and they said, 'If you're going to be a fool, we'll put you in the field and that's it.' And then they left him.

"I guess he's still a fearful horse to some degree because of that, too . . . . so, he's very sensitive to what's going on. His brain always convinces him that somebody is there to hurt him."

But no one can hurt Banker's Jet anymore. He's at Pleasant Valley, where his only assignment these days, Roy said, is to "mow and fertilize whatever pasture he's in.

More than a decade after the rescue, Ron Gibson asked about Banker's Jet. When informed of his dappled coat and idyllic surroundings, Gibson sighs. "You know," he says, "if any horse deserved to be saved, it was that one."

HOPE

An apple wafer is cupped in Darrell Smith's right hand. Slowly, the 13-year old extends his arm to a Thoroughbred christened Maybe I'm Amazed. The horse gently licks the treat off Smith's hand.

"That tickles," he says.

The child's laughter fills the shedrow in Delray Beach, Fl. It is heartfelt and joyous. It mocks the neglect that took Smith from his family and into foster care for three years. The young boy searches his pocket for another apple wafer. "You know what I like about horses?" he asks. "They're smart, friendly, and they like being around people. And if you show them affection they'll always be there for you."

And so they have for Darrell at Children, Hope & Horses, created by founder Laura Newberry to create a supportive learning environment through an interactive horse program for abused, neglected and abandoned children. And so they have for hundreds of other children at the Luci Center in Shelbyville, Ky., and Dream Catcher Stables in Spring, Tx.

"The benefits these horses provide are immeasurable," said Gay Kersh, a psychotherapist who is familiar with Sanna Roling's Dream Catcher Stables. "The children and adults get a sense of well being and pride and self-esteem. It also teaches them to trust again."

They learn to trust Affirmeds Ace, who competed for 11 years in claiming events in the midwest. Since 2002, the Ohio-bred has carried children from Dream Catcher Stables to gold medals in the Special Olympics. They've also learned to trust and care for the retired Thoroughbred Last Song, who's helped heal the physically and mentally disabled at the Luci Center.

"When you see these horses working with the children a miracle blossoms before your eyes," Roling said. "The horse is not a tool. He is the therapist. If you have an intelligent horse and you hand him over to a person with a disability, it will take him only 20 or 30 minutes to figure out the rider. The horse will realize what the rider can do for himself, and he'll cover for those things the rider can't do. And the children working with these horses will realize you can't out-muscle an animal like this. So they learn discipline and confidence and trust. They learn kindness and they soon understand unconditional love."

Donna Smith, a dance instructor who adopted Darrell in spring of 2003, says she has seen a change in her son since working with the Thoroughbreds and polo ponies at Children, Hope & Horses.

"When Darrell first moved in he didn't know what to call me," Donna said. "There were a lot of emotions going back and forth. He had another picture of who his mom was. So the first good thing about the program was our time together. I could stay with him and watch him groom the horses. That gave us stuff to talk about. He showed me things I didn't know about the horses and that was good for him.

"But I really think the horses brought out his ability to show emotion. He wasn't one to hug or anything like that. But I see an affection and bond he

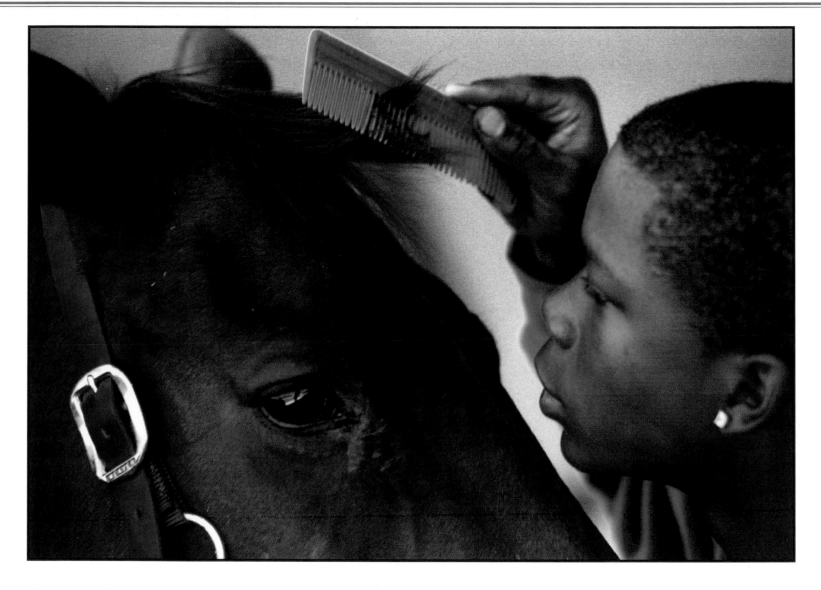

has with the horses. He communicates when he's grooming them. He's able to show physical compassion. You see him respond to the horses, and that has allowed him to hug us."

Horses like Maybe I'm Amazed "don't care if a person has a disability," said Paula Nieto, founder of the Luci Center. "A horse freely gives of himself. And the adults and children we have coming here not only get physical contact with the horses but a spiritual contact."

"I think that's what amazes me so much about horses. They can suffer at the hands of humans. But at the hand of another human they can learn to trust again. It's the same for a person, especially a child."

And so Darrell Smith moves slowly down the shedrow offering apple wafers. Like the horses, he's learning to trust again.

CLEARY

A van stops and the side doors open. A wheelchair carrying Robin Cleary is lowered down a ramp by a nurse and placed a few feet from the training track at Calder Race Course. Rays of light splinter the cobalt morning sky above Miami and a group of Thoroughbreds approach from out of the turn.

"This is what keeps me going," Cleary, 48, says as a big chestnut named Wheaton's Aly carries her husband, Brian, past in a full gallop.

"He's a handful this morning," Brian shouts from the track

"He's feeling good," she replies with a smile.

It has been eight years since Robin Cleary was first placed in this wheelchair. Eight years since she was thrown to this track when a horse she was breezing broke his front legs. A helmet protected Cleary's head but her spinal column was severed in the spill. She is a quadriplegic.

Immediately after the accident, Cleary says, "everything fell apart." It was hard to look down the shedrow at a group of horses she loved but couldn't touch. She found it hard to help Brian, a Thoroughbred trainer whom she assisted for 21 years. Horses were her whole life. It was a way to mark time. Her mother, who rode an Arabian stallion when pregnant with Robin, would tell friends her daughter rode before she was born. She met Brian at the track in 1975. He called her Ginger Rogers. He, of course, was Fred Astaire.

"When something like this happens you can do one of two things. You can give up and say, 'Well, that's it, I'm just gonna die.' Or you can decide to live," Robin says.

Robin Cleary decided to live.

She's back at the barn each morning watching the horses Brian gallops around the track, inspecting them afterward and helping to decide when they will race again. She has also become an ambassador for the Miami Project to Cure Paralysis, raising more than $500,000 solely within the Thoroughbred industry.

And she's helping children by helping horses.

Once a horse's racing career is over, the Clearys work to place their horses in loving, healthy environments. They have succeeded with Alpine Way, a 14 year-old mare residing in Delray Beach, Fla., at Children, Hope & Horses, a non profit interactive horse program that helps kids who have been sexually abused, physically assaulted, or neglected.

Like many of the children, Alpine Way's journey to this place has not been easy. A winner of two of 19 starts, Alpine Way bowed a tendon shortly before Robin's accident. "I was trying to figure out what to do with her, where she could retire, and I found a farm in Ocala where she could have a nice life," Robin said.

But the farm was sold and Alpine Way was part of the package. Several years passed before Robin learned Alpine Way had been sold and relocated to Ohio.

"She had been bred and was on a farm, but it wasn't what I wanted for her," Robin said. "She was near Lake Erie and my idea for her was to be on a big, beautiful farm where she was going to be warm. Alpine Way was always very special to me. She was a shy filly and she had bucked her shins at one point pretty badly. So I worked exclusively with her. I was pretty much the only person she was comfortable with. I rode her, rubbed her. I knew her well and I wanted her to be happy."

Robin negotiated to purchase Alpine Way. She vanned her to South Florida at her own expense and then learned of Children, Hope & Horses, located at the Sunshine Meadows Equestrian Village. "It was a perfect fit," Robin said. "She enjoys the track setting, and she likes a lot of action around her."

And she likes the children who call her by her new name - Hope.

40

44

"I don't know how to describe the communication between man and horse. But there was something about him. . . his beauty, his stature, his eyes, his demeanor. The Mexicans (at the stable) called him Guapo, which means handsome. When I couldn't care for him anymore, I took him to Tranquility (Farm). When I brought him up there he wouldn't leave me. He kept coming back to the fence. It was like leaving a kid at school the first day. They look at you like, 'Hey, don't leave me.' But now he's got his buddies. And when I go up and see him ripping across the arena. . . it's a beautiful sight to see."

Al Hansen, who purchased Baraonet, winner of $161,172, for $1, on his way to slaughter.

jamie

There was an incident in Howard County.

A racist remark was made to a pregnant black girl. Her Jewish boyfriend became enraged. A door was broken down, punches were exchanged, blood was spilled and the police were called.

"And here I am," said Jamie Elliott, hugging the retired Thoroughbred Sharp Chance behind the Charles H. Hickey Detention Center in Baltimore.

You can't see the concertina wire from the paddock behind the barn, or the chainlink fence that separates you from the single-file march of inmates outside the main brick building. But this is prison, where the uniform is orange overalls. This is where you land when you're 18 and put away for juvenile assault and malicious destruction of property. This is hell when you're locked away and you've missed the birth of your only son.

"His name is Marcus," said Elliott, who strokes his goatee with the hand from a right arm that features a prominent Star of David tattoo. "He was born three weeks ago, but I haven't seen him. I couldn't get a special visit. I get to make one phone call every week, so when I call my girlfriend she puts the phone up to his ear so he hears my voice and maybe recognizes me when I get out. You have no idea how bad I want to get out of here and see him."

Jamie Elliott is articulate and thoughtful. There seems to be high voltage crackling through him as well as a history of family dysfunction and a nomadic existence. Born in New York, he has lived in Kansas, Florida, Ohio, Wisconsin, New Jersey and Maryland. "And we lived in several towns in each of those places," he said.

After being arrested for marijuana possession when he was on the streets after his mother kicked him out of the house, Elliott tried to turn his life around. He got a job selling sporting goods and saved $600 for the birth of his son. "We bought the baby clothes and the diapers...everything was planned out perfect," he said.

Then he heard what someone said about his girlfriend. "She was pregnant, showing at the time," he recalled. "I was so pissed off I kicked the shit out of the guy."

House arrest preceded a sentence at the Hickey Center; a former orphanage that houses up to 300 juvenile offenders in Baltimore as well as three dozen Thoroughbreds from the Thoroughbred Retirement Foundation. Elliott admits he was skeptical when asked if he wanted to work with the horses.. "I'd never been around horses," he recalled. "I don't even remember seeing them when I went to the Bronx Zoo." But shortly after he agreed to work with the thoroughbreds, Sharp Chance was vanned in from Charles Town Race Track.

"He was the first horse I saw," he said of the 3-year-old Kentucky-bred colt who raced 12 times for cheap claiming purses. Elliott reaches over the fence and gently rubs the colt's neck. "I love this horse."

Sharp Chance was claimed for $5,000 in April, 2003 by Merri Toulas. But a cursory look revealed knee and ankle problems and after racing the bay gelding just once, Toulas couldn't stand to watch Sharp Chance suffer any longer.

"He was going to break down or get claimed and maybe wind up at one of those auctions where they buy horses for slaughter," Toulas said. "I didn't want that to happen to him because he's a nice, gentle horse. So I called the

Thoroughbred Retirement Foundation because I wanted him to have a good home."

Elliott was the first inmate to work with Sharp Chance at the Hickey Center. "He was standing alone in the pen next to the barn and I walked over and started petting him," Elliott recalled. "He was friendly and we just hit it off. I was the first one to walk him. The first one to bathe him. The first one to feed him. He's so gentle. He's like my best friend in here."

Elliott wants to do the right thing when he's released from the Hickey Center. He's going to go back to work at the sporting goods store, save some money and get a little apartment for his family. "I want my son to have a good home and be happy," he says. And one day, he wants to bring Marcus to the Hickey School to meet Sharp Chance.

"I want to show my son this horse," said Elliott, still holding tight to Sharp Chance. "I love this horse."

BiLL BiGGER

It's not easy finding Bill Bigger.

Twenty minutes off I-95 in Martin County, Florida - past miles of sun bleached rural roads that turn to dirt and gravel at a general store called Huck's Country Corner - Bigger stands with two horses under a shade tree at the far end of a pasture.

The tree line is low, the sky is big, and this pasture seems to run forever. Bigger tips his cowboy hat and wipes the dust from his salt-and-pepper beard before hoisting a sack of feed. Gingerly, he presents a handful to a 23-year old retired Thoroughbred gelding named Upper Star.

"Sometimes I just light a fire out here at night, listen to the radio and he comes up right next to me," Bigger says. "It's just me and him."

While serving time at the Marion Correctional Institution outside Ocala, Bigger was one of several inmates who cared for horses sent there by the Thoroughbred Retirement Foundation (TRF). Two of those horses were Upper Star and a 12-year-old gelding named Gallant Guest. Bigger developed such a powerful bond with the horses that, four months after his release, he adopted the two geldings and brought them here to this land north of Palm Beach.

"I really wanted to make sure they would always be cared for because when they came in they both had problems and I hated to see them go through the hurt," Bigger says.

Gallant Guest, a Florida-bred who raced 101 times over 15 tracks, arrived at the TRF facility at the Marion Correctional Institution aggressive and fearful. "He got off the track because he had a cracked sesamoid in his left front leg,

but they say he had been beaten by a women after that," Bigger recalls. "He really didn't trust people and it took me three weeks to get the brush past his shoulder blades. But I went slow with him because I knew he had been abused and I wanted to get that out of him."

"I remember when he first came in I told (TRF farm manager) Betty Jo Bock, 'I want him.' She said, 'Are you sure?' And I told her, 'Like a heartache.' " Upper Star, who raced mainly in New York during his five-year career, arrived with lacerations on his fetlocks. "But he's never had a mean bone in his body," Bigger says. "The only thing he'll do is nudge you when you're rubbing his head."

Bigger, raised in Charlottesville, Va., is the son of a veterinarian. "I grew up around animals," he says. "I had a horse named Cricket when I was just 10." But life took Bigger away from his first love, and it wasn't until he was imprisoned after a DUI charge that he discovered what was missing in his life.

"I loved horses ever since I was a kid," he says. "I learned to trust and respect them, but sometimes you forget how much they mean and how they can soothe you. Like Gallant. He's very verbal. He's got two squeals. One is playful. The other is what I call his basement squeal. It means, 'Watch out, something is fixin' to happen.' But every month we have full moon camp outs, go riding in the groves back here, and he has a slow, mellow walk."

As Bigger, 51, pulls more feed from the sack, Gallant Guest and Upper Star patiently stand by his side waiting for handfuls. "It's love and affection," he says from under his big hat. "Sure, they cost money. They take time. But I just let them be horses. I feed them, I shower them, and they dearly love it. To know something this big, strong and powerful can be so gentle and still understand that both of you have to work together? That's truly something."

Bigger rests his hands on Gallant Guest. "You know, these horses aren't going to replace a wife or a girlfriend. But if I fall off one, they're going to be waiting when I get up."

"Those horses have made a lot of difference in the lives of many men."

Father Peter Young

"People wear me down, but never the horses."

Kelly Young, President and Founder of Lost & Found Horse Rescue, Jacobus, PA

EFRAIN SILVA

He is standing on the dirt road that cuts through Wallkill Correctional Facility - fidgeting nervously in oversized, black galoshes while standing in a shallow puddle of mud - when raindrops begin to streak his thick eyeglasses and moisten his worried face.

Efrain Silva, short and round, looks like he's crying.

"I have to bandage that horse's foot when they're done," Silva says softly while gesturing toward Mossad, a gentle gelding who is having a cyst removed from his left front foot. "I try to do what I can for all of them. I pet them, I clean them, I wash them. I tell people they're my family in prison."

Prison has been Efrain Silva's home for twenty-two years. First Rikers then Sing Sing, Downstate and Green Haven, Silva has been at Wallkill the past eight years serving fifteen-years-to-life for murder in the second degree. He is quiet under this gunmetal sky, shy and harmless in those thick glasses and cumbersome galoshes that splash along the road. He was once a family man with a wife and three kids.

"I've been living in Manhattan," says Silva, 66, as if the clock stopped twenty-two years ago and as if he still works five days a week and takes his children on Sunday fishing trips.

So what happened? Was it love or theft? Greed or jealousy?

"I think alcohol did it," he says while looking out across a field of retired horses. "I don't consider myself an alcoholic. When I got off work I used to go have a couple drinks. On this night I overdone it."

His thoughts become fractured, his speech altered. He stares ahead as if reliving the nightmare.

"It was a gun. Somebody owed me $200. I went into the bar to try and get my money. The guy says he doesn't have the money. All he had was this gun. So he gave me the gun for the $200 he owed me. I said, 'Well, I'll take it to protect my family.' "

Silva shakes his head. He looks old and weary. This place he's forced to visit, the consequences of his act...they never change. A third of his life has gone to waste.

"I was so drunk that...it just happened. People got in my way for no reason at all. I wasn't thinking. I can't even picture it myself. I never killed anything. As a matter of fact, I love animals. The only thing I ever did was go fishing. The only thing I ever killed was fish."

His children are grown, his parents are old, and his wife is ill. Once every three months, Silva gets to spend the weekend with his wife as part of Wallkill's family reunion program. But "my family can't take it," he sighs. "I have six grandchildren that I haven't seen grow up. That's what hurts. I used to take my sons and daughter fishing, to amusement parks, and I can't do that with my grandchildren."

So these horses have become Efrain Silva's family. They are one of his few links to love and mercy. He has grown old with some of them and has developed a bond with others.

"I guess my favorite was Crème de La Fete," says Silva of a popular, New York-based gelding who raced 151 times over eight years. "He was kind and he'd respond to you. He liked people. I gave him apples and carrots and I'd take him for little walks.

"He used to love clover. You know, the sweet clover?"

Crème de La Fete spent the last sixteen years of his life at Wallkill. Described as a "gritty warrior" during his racing days and a winner of forty races, Silva cared for the gelding and treated him his final year for Cushing's Disease, a painless tumor of the pituitary gland.

"Efrain administered the medicine and tended to that horse like they were best friends," said farm manager Jim Tremper.

The gelding eventually died at 25. "It happened in the field," Silva says.

"One day he didn't eat his regular grain when I showed up. I told Jim, 'I think he's on his way out,' and he was. I was able to say goodbye, but it hurt a lot."

Silva stands on the dirt road oblivious to the mud. He squints through the raindrops on his glasses. A piece of Mossad's hoof has been cut away. The cyst has been drained and the foot is ready to be bandaged.

"I could do time if it wasn't for my family," Silva says. "We're all doing time in this world. We're born, we live the best we can, and we die. But it's hard with my family. So the horses are therapy for me. They're in need. I help them like I would help my family. See, the horses...they alleviate my hurt and pain and, in return, I try to do the best I can for them."

And then Efrain Silva walks up to Mossad, gently touches his neck and begins bandaging his foot to ease the pain.

KeLLy young

Kelly Young isn't going to New Holland.

She says that every Sunday. It's her mantra from the time she gets up until she goes to bed. "And sometimes," she says, a smile creasing her angelic face, "I almost believe it."

But then Monday morning breaks. And Kelly Young must save the horses.

It has been like this for 11 years of Mondays. The solemn, 40-minute drive on Pennsylvania roads from her farm in Jacobus. The parking lot teeming with vans, horse-drawn carriages, and the five-and-dime flea market. And then those first steps into the New Holland Sales Company.

Jesus, where do you start? How do you describe a carnival in hell? Two hundred, three hundred horses tied to metal pylons so closely you can't squeeze a halter? Children eating ice cream and old men laughing across manure-streaked concrete. Your senses are assaulted, choked with the smell of urine and hay as horses of all ages and breeds are ridden hard into a tiny auction ring surrounded by rickety, wooden bleachers. "*Bring me in another one,*" the auctioneer demands. A Thoroughbred is forced through a small chute and into the ring. A handful of 'killer buyers' examine the flesh, hoping to buy cheap and sell to slaughter.

And in the middle of the tumult stands Kelly Young. For 11 years of Mondays.

"I always say each Sunday I'm not going," Young says "But then I wake up and it's like, 'I've got to go.' If I don't go I feel like I'm letting them down. It's like an obligation to them. I might not be able to save them all, but the ones I do save, hopefully, will go on to have a second chance."

Young, 38, has saved more than 500 horses from slaughter, negotiating for their lives with the killer buyers before vanning them to her 140-year-old barn for rehabilitation and retraining. A few feet from the barn, in a small office where she and her husband, Tracy, run the Lost & Found Horse Rescue, Young is surrounded by photographs of the horses she has saved.

There's Squall Watch, a half-brother to 1999 Kentucky Derby winner Charismatic, purchased from the killer buyers for $425 and now competing in dressage events. Dollar Spot, bought for $400, competes in three-day events in the mid-Atlantic. And there's Forever Baby, retired on a farm in Virginia after Young negotiated his rescue from New Holland while he stood in the "kill pen" staring at a dead pig in the scoop of a small tractor.

"This is a very depressing job," Young admits. "But then you sit back and look at these pictures and say, 'Wow, look at what these horses are doing now.' It's amazing and that's what makes it worth while, giving them an opportunity to bring peace and joy to someone's life."

Young experienced that joy early in life when her father brought home a

Shetland pony in the back of his pickup truck. "His name was Patches and he's truly why this rescue exists," she says. "He was my first pony and my very best friend. My peace and comfort came from my companionship with him. You know, there are bonds you just can't explain sometimes between a person and an animal."

And that bond created Lost & Found, a grassroots, non-profit that exists with the help of 20 volunteers, a few small grants, and the generosity of donors. "Many like the little old lady down the street who sends $20 each month," Young says. And others like the local farmer who sent 30 bales of hay late one fall afternoon for the 25 horses waiting for adoption on Young's property.

It's hard work, running the farm and finding homes for the horses she rescues. Young spends up to eight hours each Monday at New Holland. She keeps track of how many horses are led from the auction ring into the 'kill pen,' and which 'killer buyers' will negotiate to sell. It is a numbing experience but Young doesn't see an alternative unless there is a national ban on horse slaughter.

"A lot of times people in the professional community think rescue people are do-gooders; people who don't have any history with horses," she says. "But I've had horses since I was four and I believe part of horse ownership is planning for an ending. I'm not against euthanizing a horse. What I'm against is putting a horse through slaughter.

"After all these horses do for us, shouldn't they die in an environment they're familiar and comfortable with instead of being carted off 20 hours by van to a slaughterhouse?"

So she saves the horses. As she has for 11 years of Mondays. And before she walks toward the auction ring, before she walks past the lunch counter and the killer buyers, Kelly Young says a prayer and asks that she may save those who can't save themselves.

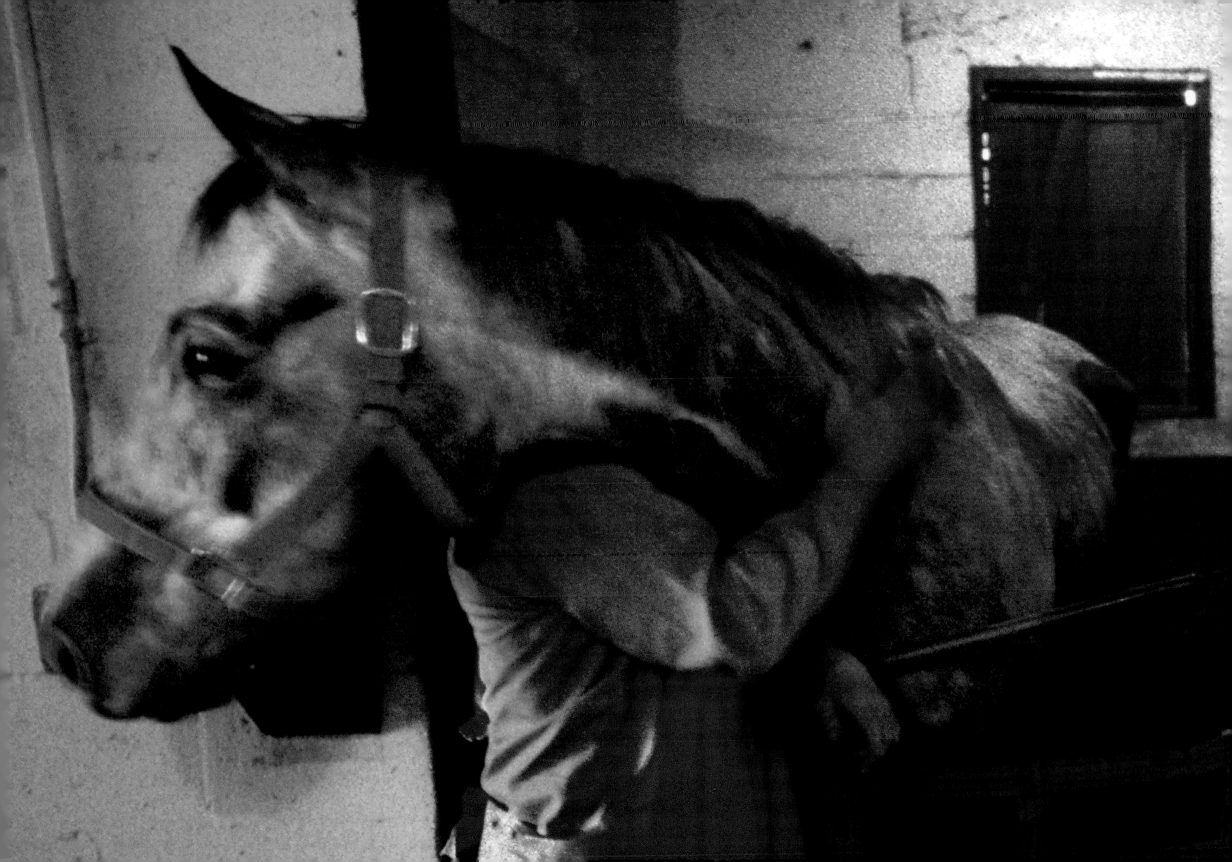

TIDAL SURGE

Shortly after driving into Whispering Willow Stables with a grocery bag full of carrots - after having weaved past traffic on the Ventura Freeway and driven past the Disney and Warner Bros., studio lots in Burbank, Ca. - Paul Wilson will announce his arrival to a 14-year-old gelding named Tidal Surge. And he doesn't have to say a word.

Just before he reaches the stall, Wilson forages into his bag and breaks a carrot in half.

Snap!

Ears straight up, Tidal Surge pokes his head from his stall. "Look at him," says Wilson, reaching up to give the compact bay gelding several carrots. "Isn't he beautiful? He loves being a horse. He loves being useful."

For the past five years this has been the beginning of a daily ritual between Wilson, a painter and filmmaker and Tidal

Surge, a stakes-winner who was rescued from neglect in Maryland. Several days a week, Wilson will spend an hour meticulously brushing Tidal Surge and feeding him carrots before slipping a saddle and saddle cloth on the gelding from the Maryland Jockey Club.

Then, before taking him for a ride in Griffith Park, Wilson will cradle Tidal Surge's head in his arms and gently, quietly, stroke the gelding's forehead for several minutes. Despite a buzz from the distant Ventura Freeway, Wilson and Tidal Surge are at peace.

"They're so used to going fast all the time, you've got to slow it down for them," Wilson says with Tidal Surge's head in his arms. "They have to trust you

beyond anything. And he trusts me and he's changed my life. Living in Hollywood, you fight that struggle every day; you don't get a break. It's a lot of bullshit. But the horse is always the same. You come to see him and he's happy to see you. It's like that puppy from the pound. Once you get involved it ends up being bigger than you ever thought it would be."

And so it has for Wilson. After adopting Tidal Surge from the Thoroughbred Retirement Foundation's farm at the Charles H. Hickey Detention Center in Maryland - after learning he was a multiple-stakes winner who was several hundred pounds underweight when rescued - Wilson became interested. He wondered how a horse who earned more than $250,000 and had collected a check in 29 of his 30 races could slip through the cracks.

"I understood he wasn't Secretariat or Seattle Slew, and I realized he wasn't a stallion," Wilson says. "But I started asking myself, 'Where do these horses go when their value is done on the track?' "

Wilson learned Tidal Surge was a Maryland-bred son of champion Little Current, winner of the 1974 Preakness and Belmont Stakes who lived to be 32. Tidal Surge had raced three years in Delaware, Pennsylvania and Maryland and before retiring in 1995 had reeled off five consecutive victories, three coming in stakes races under jockey Jeff Carle.

"He wasn't a big horse by Thoroughbred standards, but he really was all heart," said Carle, who trains Thoroughbreds in Maryland. "He had speed but he had the ability to stretch out. In the Jennings (Handicap), he was in a protracted duel with another horse. A lot of horses would have stopped at the top of the lane, but he refused to give up. He had so much courage."

He was supposed to remain in Maryland after his racing career, supposed to be safe on a farm. But when financial difficulties depleted the farm's resources, Tidal Surge and several other horses had to be rescued by Andre Wheeler of the Thoroughbred Retirement Foundation.

"We brought him (to the Hickey Detention Center) with six or seven other horses," Wheeler said. "He was kind of beat-up, skinny and underweight. He wasn't abused, but he needed his shots updated and his feet done. It wasn't too long, though, before he started coming around. And I knew with a lot of care he could be an awesome horse."

Wilson, a Maryland native who heard about Tidal Surge from a family member, became so captivated by the gelding after adopting him that he acquired videotape of his victories from the Maryland Jockey Club. He talked to Carle, and visited Little Current in Washington state. Wilson then produced a one-hour documentary titled, 'After The Race Is Run,' which chronicles a Thoroughbred from birth to retirement.

"I grew up in Maryland surrounded by horse farms," Wilson says. "I used to see them in pastures all over the place. But after a while you don't even look at them. You take them for granted. But if you take a closer look, some are just stuck out there and neglected. I guess the point of doing the documentary was to show he's just one example of the tons of others that are out there. And he's an example of one of those horses, a horse who changed someone's life."

Wilson breaks another carrot and Tidal Surge extends his neck to grab it. Today they'll ride past the barns and off into a park filled with shade trees. Today, Wilson will let him gallop and feel like a race horse.

"Isn't he beautiful?" asks Wilson, rubbing Tidal Surge's nose. "I admit it. I've fallen in love with this horse."

PRISCILLA CLARK

One, two, three, four....

A line of Thoroughbreds forms behind Priscilla Clark as she makes her way across a paddock at Tranquility Farm

Five, six, seven, eight...

Straight as a string, the Thoroughbreds wait patiently for Clark to open a gate leading from a dusty paddock to a field of thick green grass. Nobody moves on this windy October morning until Clark swings open the gate. Then, like the refined, older gentlemen they have become at Tranquility, a dozen retired geldings walk leisurely into this pasture of green.

Clark lets loose with her infectious laugh as the line passes. Then, leaning on the gate next to her constant companion, a Jack Russell christened Yoda, she begins to introduce the herd.

"Well, let's see now...right there is Sekondi, who won the Bay Meadows Derby and over $400,000," she says. "And right here is Snipledo, who also won over $400,000 and was a champion in Washington state. And there's Southern Wish. He won The Bart Handicap at Santa Anita and more than a half million."

More than two hours northwest of Santa Anita Park - past a graveyard of commercial jets in the Mojave Desert and off a winding stretch of road - Priscilla Clark is running a sanctuary for more than 80 retired race horses at the base of the Tehachapi Mountains. It is a sanctuary she hopes can be used as a template for similar sites all over North America.

The idea is a simple one: Open farms close to racetracks that provide a retirement home for abandoned, neglected or injured Thoroughbreds; farms that can also be rehabilitation centers for horses who can become jumpers, pleasure horses or work with physically and mentally challenged people.

"I want to enhance the reputation of the horse," says Clark, 57, who conducts a tour of the 40-acre farm while offering a history of each horse.

Take Southern Wish, who Clark rescued from a gulch surrounded by barbed wire. Or Giotto, an orphan impounded by the Sheriff's office after he was found starving to death. Then there's River Rhythm, a 16-year-old bay gelding ridden several times by Hall of Fame jockey Steve Cauthen. "He hates other horses and children," Clark says of the former graded-stakes winner. "He's also a dunker. Everytime you feed him his food, he dunks it in his water. He's got to make soup out of it."

Clark has been in the business of saving and rehabilitating Thoroughbreds for more than 20 years, a business she admits is often a tough sell. "It's really a stupid idea to think you're going to run a large horse farm on charity donations...it's dumber than dirt," she says smiling. "And there's an undercurrent from some people that you're crazy because you're involved in such a project."

Clark previously ran two smaller retirement farms before she made a connection with Thoroughbred owner-and-breeder Gary Biszantz. "And the odds of this happening?" she asks, gesturing at Tranquility with a sweep of her right hand. "Astronomical."

Biszantz, the principal founder of Cobra Golf and chairman of the Thoroughbred Breeders and Owners Association, heard of Clark's efforts to help Thoroughbreds and offered to purchase a farm for her to run if the price was right. After a 2 1/2-year search, Clark found Tranquility, an abandoned ranch in Cummings Valley surrounded by sod and organic vegetable farms. Biszantz bought it for $240,000.

"The first time I met Gary was when he drove up to the front gate of the farm with the realtor," Clark recalls. "We walked around the farm and he said, 'Well, what do you think?' I told him it was only a couple hours from the track, it was a good place for horses to rehab, and I think it could work. So he writes the check, gives it to the realtor, and says, 'I'll call you. Go for it.' "

Biszantz, owner of Cobra Farm in Lexington, Ky., has donated money for more than 20 years to horse rescue organizations and has been an industry leader in promoting retirement farms. To honor the memory of his father, who introduced Gary to racing, Tranquility Farm at the Harry A. Biszantz Memorial Center opened in 1998.

"The people who run these farms like Priscilla have the kind of passion that makes you want to help," Biszantz said. "I think everyone in the industry thinks farms like Tranquility are a good idea, and the idea is really a simple one. Give these horses a second chance, a second career. And most horses, given enough time to heal and be repaired, can do great things. They can become hunters and jumpers and police horses. It's an enormous opportunity for everyone."

Clark spends hours in a covered arena retraining horses who can be adopted. One is a 2-year-old named Captain's Log, a colt bred in Florida who injured his suspensory before ever making it to the track.

"He's just a baby and he's so young and immature, we're basically teaching him all over again," Clark says. "People don't understand why horses coming straight from the track can't stand still when you try to take their tack off. It's because a lot of them have been micro-managed. They've only learned to do one thing. It's like college kids who play basketball and all they know is to play basketball. They're illiterate. We try to make our horses literate and well-rounded so they can be adopted and leave here to do a number of things."

Clark had 20 horses adopted in the summer of 2003, but she says there are thousands more who could be adopted if given the opportunity. To accomplish that goal, she says, farms such as Tranquility should be established across the country so owners have a structured way to unburden themselves of horses.

She also believes slaughter must be outlawed immediately.

"We have a culture," Clark says. "It's tough for Americans to get off their asses and say, 'This is offensive to us.' We consider the horse a pet, a companion animal. It's not an agricultural commodity. It's not food.

"You know, it's just pure Darwinian, ruthless, cold-blooded, reptilian...Really, horses are just plain lucky, any kind of horse, if they make it through a normal lifespan on the planet. I don't care if they're race horses or quarter horses or mustangs. The ones that make it are blessed because the odds are they're not going to make it through all the pitfalls. It's survival of the fittest and sometimes the survival of the luckiest. It's fate, which ones get saved and which ones don't."

Clark surveys the field of horses. Some graze contently, others catch the wind in their faces.

"I guess they're subject to the same laws of the universe that we are."

sully

Tim Sullivan looks pensively out the window of his home in Woodstock, N.Y., a home shared with two cats and hundreds of books, trying to piece together his epiphany, the beginning of his journey. "Was it a Monday or a Tuesday?" he wonders as he looks at a charcoal sky.

He is soft-spoken and meticulous, a former speechwriter deliberate in his facts. "Let's see," he begins. "They ran the Clark Handicap at Churchill Downs and that's where I won some great bucks, maybe $4,500. So I have this money and I'm not thinking much about it except I'm glad I have it. Then, the following Monday, I was looking through the (Daily Racing) Form..."

Sullivan, 60, becomes more animated as he recalls the details. "Yes, it was a Monday and I was looking through the Form and I turn to the races at Suffolk Downs and I see his name."

"Lese Majeste."

Sullivan smiles as he mentions the name.

Less than a mile from Sullivan's home, tourists roam the downtown streets and patchouli wafts through the gift shops. People still visit this village to capture the muse that attracted artists like Bob Dylan and Van Morrison. But right here, right now, Sullivan is still trying to figure out what drew him to the name of one horse in a tabloid filled with the names of hundreds of horses. What made him spend all the money he had won making sure an 11-year-old gelding who raced 190 times could finally be retired to a safe, loving home?

"There may have been something like an epiphany," Sullivan says, choosing his words carefully. "The name...the dismal record...the age...I had this sense, and that may have been the epiphany, this sense that called to mind so many

other wonderful horses that went from being allowance winners, occasional minor-stakes winners, who plummeted all the way to $3,500 claiming races and finally nothing more would ever be heard about them again."

Lese Majeste was approaching that point. For nine years, the Kentucky-bred gelding had toiled in claiming races; first New York, then Florida, and, for the past seven years, the cheaper tracks in New England. On the day Sullivan looked at his past performances in the Daily Racing Form, Lese Majeste hadn't won in more than a year. In his last six starts, run in the span of 42 days, Lese Majeste had earned $800.

Sullivan, who has bet the races for more than 50 years, knew Lese Majeste was serving a purpose. "A lot of horses hang in a lot longer than they might because they fill (racing programs)," he says. "They're immediate throw-outs, they don't complicate the betting and every once in a while they may grab a piece of the (purse)."

But Sullivan was also becoming aware of efforts by several organizations to save such horses, to make sure their final days aren't spent in cramped vans traveling from auction to auction before having their throats slit in a slaughterhouse in a remote town in Texas or Mexico or Quebec.

"I'd read from time-to-time about horses being retired to schools or hospitals or prisons, places one wouldn't associate with horse retirement," Sullivan says. "The operating theory was that frequently, souls who are in these places, people who are frightened or disturbed, get great pleasure and companionship that they can't sometimes create with other human beings.

"I thought, 'You've got this money in your pants. Why don't you just take a stab at seeing if you can get this horse.' "

Sullivan e-mailed Suffolk Downs asking for information on purchasing and retiring a horse. Track announcer Larry Collmus read it. "I saw the e-mail and thought it was great," Collmus recalled. "Here was a horse that had earned so much, had won so many races a few years back, and now might have a home once he's retired."

Collmus set up a meeting between Sullivan and Carlos Figueroa, the colorful trainer of Lese Majeste. Figueroa is known as 'King of the Fairs' for his dominance of the New England fair circuit in the 1970s and '80s. Within two weeks, Sullivan had not only purchased Lese Majeste, but two others horses from Figueroa's barn - Dignify and Before the Race.

"We toured Suffolk," Sullivan remembers, "it was a rainy and cold day. I saw Lese Majeste and I said to him, "I don't want to bet on you. I want to buy you and send you to a place where you'll look less miserable.' He was kind of disconsolate, at least to me. Carlos was very charming. He also must have thought, 'Gee, where do these people come from?' I'm a wise guy from New York and well aware of the fact that Carlos knows he's kicking my ass with this deal. He must have thought, 'Wow, a Christmas present.' "

Figueroa laughed at Sullivan's recollection of the meeting. "I was hoping he wouldn't leave," he said. "In fact, I was hoping he'd keep coming back."

After spending $2,000 for the three horses, Sullivan had to figure out where to send them. He had enough money to van Lese Majeste from Boston to Tranquility Farm in California. The Thoroughbred Retirement Foundation stepped in to help with the other two. "They were great," Sullivan recalls. "Simply taking over and getting vets to treat the horses and finding good homes for them."

Collmus says Sullivan's act encouraged others to get involved in Thoroughbred retirement in the New England area. "I think it inspired people." Sullivan is reluctant to claim credit. His deed was unselfish and pure. He wished only to see an aging horse retired to a good home. And what a home it is. Sullivan traveled to California a year later to see Lese Majeste at Tranquility Farm.

"It was wonderful to see him interested in having a good time," Sullivan says. "It must have been a strange experience to be in a place where you weren't yanked out every two weeks to the racetrack and were just allowed to be a horse. It was wonderful to see him in that environment and how he had been transformed by the loving care he was receiving."

Tim Sullivan is silent for a moment. The wind sweeps the trees outside his window and the cats move gingerly inside his living room. Yes, Tim Sullivan confirms, his journey began on a Monday.

DEGAGE

He holds the X-ray to the light, turning and creasing it against the barn window until a stream of colors-burnt orange, red and green-shoot through the image like a kaleidoscope. "One last look," thought Steve Murtough. He turns the X-ray for nearly a minute more until he accepts, at last, that he can no longer twist his fate.

"See the fracture?" He puts the piece of film down and looks across the barn at the beautiful chestnut colt now being coddled and rubbed by a group of inmates at the Marion Correctional Institution outside Ocala, Florida. "He's a good-looking son of a gun," Murtough adds. "He was the outfit. He was going to be my everything."

Two years before at Keeneland, Murtough purchased this colt as a yearling. Shiny as a new penny, alert and athletic, he christened his "everything" Degage. "You know, like what a dancer does," says Murtough, a slightly disheveled horseman who extends his leg and points his toe as gracefully as a Baryshnikov might, if he were wearing baggy jeans and work boots.

He put all of his money into Degage. He broke, galloped and trained him. "Everyone who got on this horse talked about how nice he was," Murtough says. "They talked about what great action he had, how he went so smooth. I had a nice horse and all of a sudden . . ."

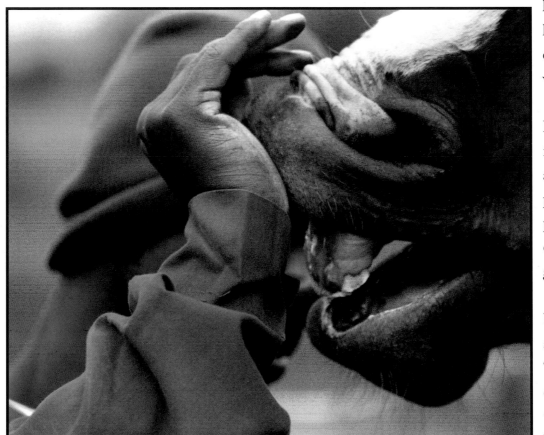

Murtough entered the barn one morning at Tampa Bay Downs and Degage just wasn't right. Then, he got the X-ray. Both sesamoids on the right hind leg were fractured. "I don't know what happened," Murtough shrugs. "Maybe there was a loose horse in the shedrow, maybe Degage hits the wall and hits it just right. I mean, he could have hit the wall a thousand times and not caused this kind of damage again. This was one in a million."

Murtough did what he could for Degage. He rested him for thirty days; fed him and rubbed him and iced him and made sure he was in as little pain as possible. He treated him like the champion he might have been. "I went broke on this horse. I just took a job as a groom at Monmouth (Park)."

The newly-minted groom paces back-and-forth. He checks on Degage and offers advice to his new handlers. The inmates are giving the colt handfuls of ice chips--"He's always loved ice"--and they walk him in circles as his stall is being prepared. "Make wider circles so he doesn't favor his leg," Murtough instructs. The colt is doing fine. It's the man who's anxious. He's chatting nervously about hope and loss for no other reason than to delay the inevitable.

He could have sold him; could have taken a thousand and cut his losses and let someone else worry about him. "But I have a duty to him," Murtough says. "I could have run him down to the stockyard auctions. He walks pretty sound and someone would have bought him. But once they started working him, he'd go lame. Then they'd run him through the same auction. Once he goes through the auction two or three times, nobody is going to buy him except the killers. And for these animals . . . that's disgusting. I couldn't do it to him. Listen, I don't doubt somebody's bought a horse off me and five, ten years down the road, they might have wound up (with the killers). But by donating a horse here, I can control that. It's not going to happen."

Murtough checks his watch--dusk isn't far off--then he looks straight ahead at Degage, who is still contentedly crunching ice out of an inmate's hand. The colt is relaxed. He's in no pain. "And that's all I want. I just want him to

be taken care of. I want him to be happy."

Inmate Brian Hughes cradles a cat in his arms while studying Murtough from afar. "A lot of people don't say goodbye," Hughes says. "Some don't even get out of their van when they leave a horse."

But Murtough has to say goodbye. Duty-bound, he resignedly moves toward "his everything." The inmates take a step back. After patting him several times, Steve Murtough buries his head in Degage's neck and grabs hold of the colt as a child would a teddy bear.

"You're going to be fine here," Murtough whispers. His voice cracks and tears well.

LORENZO PARKER

You can't appreciate the enormousness of Lorenzo Parker from a distance. Not from 200 yards away. Not when the only part of him peeking over the tall grass in a paddock at Wallkill Correctional Facility is his shaven head.

But watch him as he approaches. He's as big as the gray mare he's leading out of the paddock. You extend your hand and it disappears in Parker's paw. Big, brawny and bald. In his previous life, "I was a bully," says Parker, his intimidating presence proving the role couldn't have been a stretch.

He then goes through his history without emotion. "Born in Harlem...Family of five...Deceased father, working mother... Hanging out in the streets...Nobody paying any attention...Got trapped in the wrong crowd."

He's 39 and this is his second stint in prison. Selling drugs the first time, armed robbery the second. He was divorced a year ago. "Three kids and two grands," he says. And then he stops. Silence. You wonder if there's anything left inside the big man. Don't push them to talk, someone said. The mare Parker is holding lifts her head and lays it across his massive shoulder. And then he begins.

"I remember when I was a kid. I used to sneak out the window, get a bunch of stray dogs, use my sister's jump rope for a leash and walk them around all day. I liked dogs and, you know, they were pretty similar to these horses when they come in all skinny and messed up.

"I'd see stray dogs when I was a kid and figured I had to feed them. Me and a few of my friends would do that. We'd catch a whole lot of stray dogs, find an abandon apartment in an abandon building, then we'd put them in there and steal food out of our houses to feed them. We'd get their weight up

and then we'd take them to the park and play with them. Then, every night, we'd put them in that same damn apartment and keep taking care of them.

"That's why I don't understand why people do the things they do to these horses. If they don't want the horse no more, why don't they just give it to somebody instead of starving them and abusing them and letting them get all sick? When they can't run no more they want to abandon them and mistreat them. They enjoy their wealth and get rid of them. I say if you make $500,000 off a horse you should take care of them. If a horse made me $500,000, I'm going to buy a nice little house with a little piece of field for him."

Lorenzo Parker admires a mare grazing in front of him.

"You know what I like about these horses? They're fun, they make you laugh, and you get to hug them up."

NORTHERN STEAM

What kind of hell did Northern Steam survive?

When the frigid wind cut like a razor in the Alaskan wilderness, when the ground froze under sheets of snow and darkness suffocated daylight for weeks, was Northern Steam a victim of haunted episodes?

Was he beaten or caressed? Loved or abused?

"I only wish I knew what happened," says Sally Clampett, president of Alaska Equine Rescue.

Nobody knows the story of Northern Steam. At least not the undocumented years. There's a paper trail to trace a Thoroughbred's career on the track but it's left to fate once they stop racing. And fate was cruel to Northern Steam before he turned up in September, 2002 at the doorstep of veteran Iditarod racer Bud Smyth. He was introduced to a horse who was 300 pounds underweight and had rope burns on his legs.

"I got a call asking if I wanted a horse I could use as food for my sled dogs," Smyth says from his home in Big Lake, a village approximately 60 hard road miles from Anchorage. "They told me he was sick and crippled and had kidney stones."

How Northern Steam wound up in Big Lake at the age of 11 is a mystery. A winner of 10 of 60 races in Canada and California, the gelding's recorded history ends in November 1999 when he raced for $2,500 in Lethbridge,

Alberta, 1,600 miles from Big Lake.

"He was a nice horse," says Phil Wiest, 'Steamers' last trainer. "He had a lot of gas, a lot of speed. He had a rupture on his belly at the end and I sold him to someone who was going to lay him up and then try and run him again."

And that's when Northern Steam falls off the radar. Clampett says she believes the gelding wound up in the wilderness working for hunting guides "An outfitter dropped him off in Big Lake so he was probably part of a pack string," she says. "My God, it would have been horrible country. The horses go to very, very far away places, way up in the national parks, carrying huge loads for people hunting for moose, caribou and bear. We've had some come back emaciated."

It's not unusual in Alaska to put down a suffering animal with a bullet. "It's very quick," Clampett says. And feeding the body to sled dogs or other animals helps with disposal, especially in the winter when the ground is frozen. Smyth was ready to do such a thing in the fall of 2002.

"I figured I'd have to destroy him," Smyth says. "I was told he had been with an outfitter, in with a bunch of pack horses, draft horses...horses probably all bullying him. But when I looked at him I thought to myself, 'Who could shoot this horse?' I've been around horses and this wasn't an ordinary

Thoroughbred. They're usually hard to handle, but he was pretty docile, like a dog or cat. I thought he could be useful to somebody."

So Smyth called animal control, which in turn called Alaska Equine Rescue. What Clampett inherited was a horse 300 pounds underweight with bladder stones, according to Dr. John-Edd Brown at the Alaskan Equine and Small Animal Hospital.

"He was straining to pee and he was fairly uncomfortable," Brown says. "He was in pretty bony shape and we knew the rescue would be a salvage operation. But I was adamant about getting the (bladder) stones out. They were a little bigger than a golf ball; probably the size of a racquetball. So we performed the surgery in about an hour and a half, going through the urethra at the brim of the pelvis.

"You know, I was excited about the surgery because he was a pretty cool horse. He was kind of sour at first, he didn't want to be messed with. But once he felt better and realized everyone was trying to help him, he never struggled after that. He allowed you to work with him."

Northern Steam recuperated but his journey wasn't over. Since the gelding was unable to withstand weight because of a shattered sesamoid bone, Clampett contacted the Thoroughbred Retirement Foundation (TRF) in hopes of sending 'Steamer' to one of their satellite farms. Several months later, Northern Steam was vanned 2,800-miles to his new home at the Out 2 Pasture farm in Jamestown, Missouri.

"He's a remarkable horse," says Robin Hurst.

Hurst, a professor of biology at the University of Missouri, runs Out 2 Pasture with husband Zac March, a professor at the school's College of Veterinary Medicine. The farm is used by the school for non-terminal studies, and 'Steamer' has become a hit with students.

"We let the new students work with 'Steamer' because he's so patient and easy to deal with," Hurst says. "He's got five buddies in his herd and he's in beautiful condition. He has his needs. He gets medication twice a day so he remains pain free due to his bad stifles and his sesamoid, but what a spirit he has.

"If I was put through half as much as what he was, I don't think I would be so amendable. But he has great resiliency and he's very forgiving. And you know what else? He has great dignity."

john hettinger

The spark creates a flame and John Hettinger studies the blaze at the end of his lighter before feeding the bowl of his pipe. The smoke wafts throughout Hettinger's study, a comfortable room with a fireplace, crowded bookshelves and walls adorned with pictures of horses, hunting dogs and caricatures of Hettinger through various stages of life.

The pistol on the corner table?

"It's probably from the Revolutionary War," he replies.

This room, much like Hettinger, is elegant and noble. It is a gentleman's study on a 700-acre New York Thoroughbred farm built in 1789. It's as comfortable as the armchair Hettinger has slipped into and as familiar as the aroma of tobacco. It is an ideal place to rest and reflect...or wage a significant battle in time and money against the slaughter of horses.

"As long as I'm living," says Hettinger, 70, punctuating his words with the wave of a smoldering pipe, "I will fight the slaughter, the gruesome death, of these animals."

Hettinger has been at the forefront of this fight, whether it's helping to fund legislation to ban slaughter in the United States or creating charities to raise awareness and support adoption programs. He has written letters and made phone calls to industry leaders and politicians and donated land and money to rescue organizations.

"He's been the driving force behind us," said Chris Heyde, spokesperson for the Society for Animal Protective Legislation, a Washington based lobbying group that has helped draft legislation to ban slaughter. "His position within the

(Thoroughbred) industry, his ability to help find sponsors for bills, has allowed us to take the issue out of the humane community and bring it to the entire public."

This fight makes perfect sense for Hettinger, who grew up on this farm christened Akindale. He has owned horses since he was a 10-year-old boy.

"Alfred Vanderbilt once said he liked horses and loved racing," Hettinger says. "It's the opposite for me."

He has been immersed in Thoroughbred racing for three decades as a breeder and competitor. There are approximately 70 horses on the farm, including 20 broodmares and 20 horses in training.

Yet, despite his long involvement in racing, despite being chairman of the Grayson-Jockey Club Research Foundation and Fasig-Tipton, one of the largest Thoroughbred sales companies in the world, Hettinger admits he didn't get preoccupied with trying to stop horse slaughter until 2000.

"I can't say I didn't know what was going on," Hettinger says. "Every time I'd sell a yearling colt I'd say, 'Good luck.' It was the type of thing I shoved in the back of my mind. But a few years ago Diana Pikulski (of the Thoroughbred Retirement Foundation) came out to talk to me about the issue. I didn't have any idea of the number of horses being slaughtered and I became increasingly repulsed the more I learned about what was going on. So I've been spending my time and effort since on legislation to ban slaughter."

Hettinger has helped a number of ways. He donated his 300 acre Exceller

Farm to the Thoroughbred Retirement Foundation to be used as a re-training facility for rescued and abandoned Thoroughbreds. He has attempted to find every horse he has ever sold and has a standing offer to pay double the killer buyer's price. He has also created Blue Horse Charities, in which Fasig-Tipton will match a commitment from the buyer or consignor of any horse sold at any of its sales up to one quarter of one percent. That money is used to create awareness and help fund rescue organizations.

Hettinger is passionate about his fight and disgusted by the argument that slaughter is necessary to prevent horses from being neglected and abandoned. He also dismisses the arguments that a ban on slaughter will cost horse farms tax exemptions or create a market for stolen horses that will be shipped to slaughterhouses in Canada or Mexico.

"I've heard all their arguments for slaughter," Hettinger says. "The dumbest I ever heard was so they're not mistreated. I usually don't dignify that argument by countering it. There were 350,000 horses slaughtered in 1990 and that was down to 40,000 in 2002. Now can you tell me that (reduction) created a dramatic increase in neglect and cruelty?"

As for the argument that horses are livestock, no different than cattle and pigs? "A horse is nothing like a cow," says Hettinger, his voice rising. "There was a picture of a Budweiser Clydesdale without a halter doing an intricate maneuver the other day at Madison Square Garden. Show me a cow that can do that."

"This is something you can't hide from, something you can't cover up and pretend isn't there. An ex-president and some cardinals know the (cost) of a cover-up."

Hettinger knows the statistics by heart. He pulls from his desk copies of letters urging a ban that have been sent to legislators and slaughter apologists. Four years into this fight and the topic still churns Hettinger's stomach and still burns deep within.

Has he ever been to an auction where horses are sold to 'killer buyers?' Hettinger shakes his head from side-to-side. Has he ever witnessed the smuggled videos from the slaughterhouses? "I don't think I could ever stomach that."

"To put them through that terror...." Hettinger says. "I have nothing against euthanasia. It's done in peaceful surroundings, at home...it's like going to sleep. We owe them that much. But why put them through that terror of slaughter for what comes out to be (the cost) of three days of training? That's shameful. There has got to be a realization that putting a horse through that final week of his life, of loading and unloading at auctions until the killer buyer builds a load, to travel as long as 28 hours on a van without food and water with some winding up dead before they get to the slaughterhouse, is horrible. To put another face on it would be wrong. And there are no American interests involved.

"You know, I don't want to hurt anyone, but I want to wish them a bon voyage and I want them to get the hell out of here."

Hettinger realizes he has a struggle on his hands. He understands there will be thousands of horses slaughtered before there is an end to the fight. But from behind a cloud of smoke, Hettinger says he is prepared.

"This is my 70th year and I've had a lot of fun with the horses. I've gotten great pleasure from them. But I can't think of anything that would give me greater pleasure than to help shut down the slaughterhouses in America."

Phantom On Tour

The face of Thoroughbred retirement lives in the shadow of the historic Twin Spires.

He has a pale blaze running down his nose, four white socks and a fondness for peppermints. His paddock at the Kentucky Derby Museum in Louisville is a few hundred yards away from the main track at Churchill Downs, where in 1997 he valiiantly fought the length of the stretch to finish an admirable sixth in the 13-horse Kentucky Derby.

But like so many retired Thoroughbreds, Phantom On Tour could have been like tens of thousands of horses who wind up slaughtered each year for human consumption abroad. The fact he competed in the world's greatest race and earned more than $700,000 couldn't save him from a precipitous fall from grace.

Nearly three years after being retired because of nagging injuries and multiple ankle surgeries, Phantom On Tour raced for chump change at a minor-league track in Pennsylvania.

A champion forgotten.

The story of Phantom On Tour, says Diana Pikulski, executive director of the Thoroughbred Retirement Foundation (TRF), "incorporates so many of the problems these horses face and what we're really all about."

"Because here you had a Kentucky Derby horse, a really nice horse, who wound up forgotten and going down the wrong path. A horse basically on the

road to the slaughterhouse."

Phantom On Tour deserved so much more. The flashy red colt won two stakes in 1996 to establish himself as an early contender for the Kentucky Derby. And after winning the Rebel Stakes at Oaklawn Park in Arkansas and finishing second in the Arkansas Derby the following winter, Phantom On Tour had earned a trip to Louisville.

In the 1997 Kentucky Derby under jockey Jerry Bailey, Phantom On Tour gave a determined, gutsy effort. Racing close to a brisk pace, he fought through the stretch despite tiring to finish a game sixth behind winner Silver Charm.

After the Derby, Phantom On Tour had surgery for bone chips in his ankle and didn't race again that year. But in 1998 he came back to win the New Orleans Handicap and finish third in the Oaklawn Handicap. He was good enough to compete against some of the top handicap horses in the country but could not outrun bad ankles and a tendon injury. Unable to race any longer, owner Cal Partee sold Phantom On Tour as a stallion prospect to prominent trainer Noel Hickey.

The story should end there with the old warrior safe at home, pampered for life. But when Phantom On Tour proved to be infertile, he was gelded and sold to interests in Connecticut as a potential show horse. When that didn't work out, Phantom On Tour was sold again and, nearly three years after being retired, he showed up at Penn National Race Course. He finished eighth beaten by nearly 13 lengths. Seven weeks later, Phantom On Tour was beaten again in a race at Charles Town in West Virginia.

Kelly Danner, corporate racing manager at Churchill Downs, was told by a friend that Phantom On Tour was racing again. "I brought up the charts of his race and I was irate," Danner recalled. "I couldn't believe someone would race him again. It wasn't right."

Danner notified the staff at Churchill Downs about Phantom On Tour's plight and asked that money be raised to properly retire the horse. The TRF, in the process of forming a relationship with Churchill Downs to have a resident Thoroughbred retired at the Museum, was also contacted.

"We tried to have the current owner (Ed Price) donate him," Pikulski says. "He said he had time and money invested in the horse and he wanted something. That's when everyone got together and started raising money."

Calder Race Course in Miami, Florida, a member of Churchill Downs Inc., raised $3,000. Employees at Churchill raised several hundred dollars and the TRF raised additional money. Just weeks after getting beaten by nearly 17 lengths on Oct. 31 at Charles Town, Phantom On Tour was shipped to the TRF's farm at the Blackburn Correctional Facility in Lexington, Ky., to be evaluated. A few months later, Phantom On Tour was at his new home in the shadow of the Twin Spires.

With the exception of a few months a year when he returns to Blackburn for some down time, Phantom On Tour lives in a barn and paddock in the back of the Derby Museum. Once a week he's taken out and allowed to gallop across the track at Churchill Downs. Most days you can see him just inside Gate 2 off Central Avenue.

"He's a good looking horse with a big lazy streak," said Alison Paynter, who cares for Phantom On Tour at the Museum. "You do not disturb him when he's taking a nap. But he's a good horse and he's smart. We took him to the front door of the Museum a couple times to greet people and he'd beg for peppermints. Some people send treats, but I usually mix it in his feed. And someone at Christmas sent a candy cane. The rest of the time he's just taking it easy."

Julie Koenig, director of communications with Churchill Downs, calls Phantom On Tour "our spokeshorse for the Greener Pastures program we launched with the TRF to help retired race horses."

"He's living proof that partnerships can work and that we're all responsible for these horses," she added.

On Dec. 13, 2001, once Phantom On Tour had been removed from Charles Town and was safely in the possession of the TRF, Kelly Danner sent an e-mail to those responsible for saving the gelding. In part, the message read, "Let's make this horse a daily reminder that those who feed us, clothe us and entertain us need our help each and every day, all over the country."

"When you become older, you become wiser, right? So now I'm supposed to be wiser. I know it's complicated. I know it's not Utopia. But I want to help younger people to realize how great this sport is and how great God and nature was to give you an animal like this. I think we all want the best for these horses. That's the way it should be, right? It's the Sport of Kings. So how bad could it be to try and stop slaughter? How bad could it be to get a horse to the Thoroughbred Retirement Foundation?

Two-time Kentucky Derby-winning trainer Nick Zito, Spokesperson for the National Horse Protection Coalition

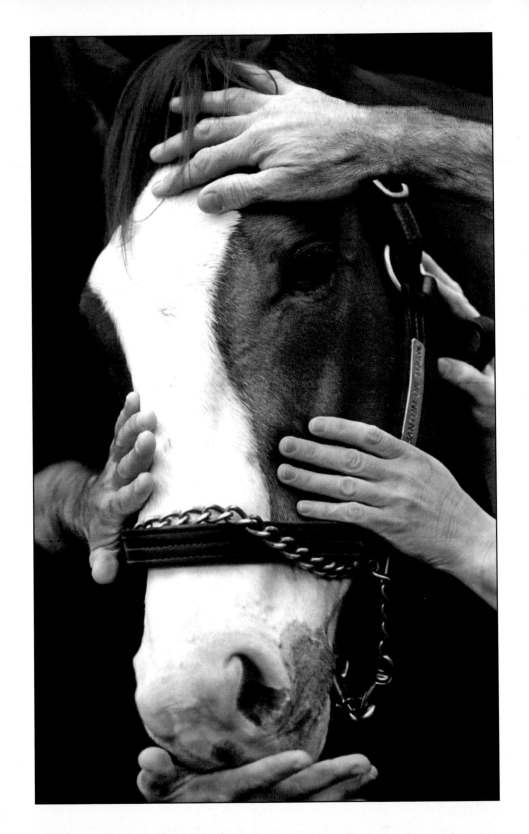

109

CAPTIONS